C0-AVO-277

GERMAN EXPRESSIONISTS

THE BLUE RIDER SCHOOL

Introduction by
OLGA NEIGEMONT

Translated from the German by
WILLIAM PERNHALL

CROWN PUBLISHERS, INC. - NEW YORK

LIST OF COLOR PLATES

THE BLUE RIDER

The ebullient intellectual atmosphere that reigned in Munich at the turn of the century attracted art lovers from all over the world to that charming city of partly rural, partly cosmopolitan character. " Everybody painted — or poetized, or made music, or studied dancing. Each house had at least two studios under its roof, where sometimes not too much painting but always a great deal of discussing, disputing, and philosophizing was practiced. Schwabing — Munich's Montmartre — was an intellectual island in the big world, in Germany, and mostly, in Munich itself," remarked the painter Wassily Kandinsky, who had arrived from Moscow in 1896, only shortly after his compatriots Alexej von Jawlensky and Marianne von Werefkin, and hoped, like them, to develop his artistic skill in the Bavarian metropolis.

It was the creative climate of Schwabing that inspired Kandinsky's thoughts of Pure Painting and Pure Art. He groped for analysis, searched for relationships, and dreamed of the " Great Synthesis." Soon, Kandinsky felt a compelling need to share his thoughts with like-minded artists. He became chairman of the independent artists' organization Phalanx and finally founded with Jawlensky, Gabriele Münter, Kandoldt, Kubin, Erbslöh, Marianne von Werefkin, and others the New Artists Association, which, due to his efforts, was soon joined by those who rejected imitation and tradition. Among the new members were Bechtejeff, the brothers Burljuk, Erma Bossi, Sacharoff, Kogan, Girieud, Le Fauconnier, Otto Fischer, Mogilewsky, and Franz Marc.

The first exhibition of the New Artists Association took place in the winter of 1909-1910. The catalogue of the paintings was preceded by the founding manifesto of the group. It states that the painters of the association would proclaim the thought that the artist — aside from his impressions of the outer world — is constantly subjected to experiences of an inner world, and that it is necessary to free oneself from incidentals and to strive for the mutual penetration of all experiences in a new artistic synthesis. Although this thought was not entirely new, and not too revolutionary for the "painting of the future," it still represented a rejection of German Impressionism and its Secessionist supporters.

To their second exhibition the New Artists Association invited the innovators Picasso and Braque, the dynamic Rouault, the color-conscious van Dongen, the unruly Vlaminck, and the more level-headed Derain. There was no clearly defined program but the exhibition proved beyond doubt that the new movement was hardly confined to Germany; that its spiritual fathers had been Cézanne, Gauguin, van Gogh, Matisse, and Picasso, and that there was also a bond with the archaic and Scythian Plastic. Even at this early stage, the future development of modern art was clearly defined in Kandinsky's statement: " To speak of the mystery through the mystery. Is not that the essence? "

The methodically inclined Kandinsky also visualized the creation of an almanac, a project he had dreamed of even before the founding of the New Artists Association. The yearbook was to be " exclusively authored by artists," and he thought especially of a collaboration between painters and musicians, " because the damaging separation of one art from the other, and further, of 'art' from folk and children's art and from 'ethnography,' erected walls between what I considered as strongly related and often identical manifestations; in one word, the synthetic connections would leave me no peace ". As strange as it seems today, Kandinsky's idea met for a long time with indifference and even rejection until he became acquainted with Arnold Schönberg, the creator of the twelve-tone technique, who accepted his plan with enthusiasm. Shortly thereafter, the decisive meeting between Kandinsky and Franz Marc took place; both artists understood each other immediately. With the help of the publisher Piper, who had been won over by Marc, the idea of the almanac became a reality in the summer of 1909. The yearbook was titled *The Blue Rider* after one of Kandinsky's paintings. He says the following about it: " We invented the name 'The Blue Rider' at the coffee table on the garden veranda in Sindelsdorf; we both loved blue Marc, — horses, I, — riders. The name suggested itself. And the fabulous coffee served by Frau Maria Marc tasted even better."

When Kandinsky and his friends severed their relationship with the New Artists Association in 1911, the small group identified itself with the name of the almanac. The split came over a difference of opinion about " the exemption from any jury," which some artists had demanded for their paintings. Marc, Kubin, and Gabriele Münter resigned together with Kandinsky. On December 18, 1911, the Blue Riders opened their own show at the Tannhauser Gallery. They exhibited 43 paintings by Kandinsky, Münter, Marc, Macke, Campendonck, Epstein, Kahler, Bloch, David and Wladimir Burljuk, Bloé-Niestlé, the composer Schönberg, and the French guests Delaunay and Henri Rousseau, *" Le Douanier."* The goal of the group is defined in the exhibition's catalogue, which stated there is no intention to proclaim any precise or special form, but rather " to show in the diversity of the represented forms how many variations the artist's inner desire creates." This meant in the last analysis the renewal of the arts through the spirit.

Three months after their first exhibition, the Blue Riders arranged their second show, this time at the Goltz Gallery. It was limited to woodcuts and drawings. Participants were the members of the "Bridge" as well as Paul Klee, Derain, Malewitsch, Emil Nolde, Morgner, Arp, Braque, and Picasso. In spite of stylistic diversity, this exhibition was a manifestation of the *avant-garde* artists' intellectual concord and solidarity. Both exhibitions were of extraordinary importance for the development of modern painting in Germany and brought the Blue Riders public recognition. They were on their way to power, to winning new friends and followers, to fortifying their position. Paul Klee had joined in 1912; Lyonel Feininger was invited in 1913 to exhibit with them at the First German Autumn Salon, which had been arranged by Herwarth Walden. About the same time as Apollinaire in France, the Blue Riders turned to a new field which until then had remained unnoticed in the arts. They focused attention on paintings by peasants in the Alps and in Russia, as well as on children's drawings; searched for the origin of artistic creativity, stood in the forefront of the era's intellectual leadership — they reasoned, analyzed, speculated. The members of the group knew that they faced a precarious future, but did not hesitate to accept their share of responsibility. They felt like pioneers of a new world whose revolutionary changes they clearly perceived. Franz Marc expressed it like this: " In the twentieth century we will live among strange faces, new pictures, and unheard-of sounds. Many who lack the inner fire will freeze and feel nothing but a chill. They will flee to the ruins of their memories. Woe to the demagogues who will want to pull them out of there! Everything has its time and the word has time."

To be sure, the time of the Blue Riders was quite limited. With the outbreak of World War I, the creative group came to a sudden end. Kandinsky, Jawlensky, and the other Russian artists had to leave Germany; Marc and Macke enlisted; Klee was attached to a military home base from 1916 to 1918; and Gabriele Münter also left the country.

The Blue Rider movement was condemned to remain the fragment of an idea but influenced, in modified form, the painting of the Bauhaus in Weimar and Dessau after 1918.

If we consider the contributions of the individual artists to the Blue Rider movement, we must name in the first place Wassily Kandinsky, who had fought for a long time and with undiminished persistence, to arouse Munich's interest in his efforts. Today we know that Kandinsky's views marked a new era in modern painting. He demanded the autonomy of forms and colors because he had recognized their independent effect from the painted subject. He writes in his autobiography: "I felt with growing clarity that the subject's inner being fulfills its form. I experienced more and more the division between art and nature until I was able to view each for itself and totally different from the other." Kandinsky went much further than all those before him who had taken the same road. With his theory and its application to painting he laid the foundation of absolute art.

The year 1910 was an important turning point in Kandinsky's artistic development. He painted his first abstract picture and wrote his book *On the Intellectual in the Arts,* which justifies his own painting, and modern painting in general, in a brilliant formulation. He states there that the new art form shows two similarities with the forms of past periods, which are, however, diametrically opposed. "The first is external," he explains, "and has therefore no future. The second is inward and carries therefore the seed of the future. After the period of materialistic temptation, which seemingly conquers the soul but is shaken off in the end, the soul rises — refined through struggle and suffering. Cruder emotions, like fear, joy, sadness, etc., which could equally serve during the period of temptation, will henceforth have little attraction for the artist. He will search for more refined emotions which are as yet nameless. He, himself, lives a complex, relatively refined life, and the work emanating from it will definitely convey finer emotions to the spectator who is able to experience them — emotions that cannot be captured in words." At a very early stage Kandinsky already felt that he was distracted and even disturbed by the subjects he painted. The shrinking of the thematic subject and, consequently, the creation of abstract painting, can therefore be considered as a logical development. He separated himself from nature so that his painting would conform only to the "inner necessity." In spite of his decision, Kandinsky remained open minded toward all other ideas. The painting of the Blue Riders served him later on, at the Bauhaus in Weimar, as a starting point for his more advanced teaching activities. Kandinsky applied his ideas of a total autonomy of the arts, in which intuition became the most essential tool for capturing and representing a world that was treated as an entity. That autonomy demanded the maximum of form and color by calling for their cerebral qualities. Next to Kandinsky, it was the contemplative Franz Marc who did most to advance the intellectual growth of the artists belonging to the Blue Riders. It was also he who, together with Arnold Schönberg, had recognized Kandinsky's advanced thinking and had come to the aid of his friend. "I found in this unforgettable man," wrote Kandinsky later, "the rare example of an artist who could look far beyond the limitations, of 'organized busybodies,' and who, not overtly but inwardly, took a stand against binding, hampering traditions." Like Kandinsky, Franz Marc was possessed of a creative sincerity that soon lifted him above the traditional norms in painting. He attempted to disassociate himself from the "indiscriminate use of color" and wanted to restore its expressive, symbolic powers, which was also Kandinsky's aim. Marc, however, because of his deep searching nature, took another path than Kandinsky and always retained a strong need for balance and a feeling for orderliness. Next to color, he was mainly concerned with form. He stated once: "The thought of an art of 'pure forms' emerged years ago — unpretentiously, almost hopelessly." In fact, his own justifications — hidden behind sophisms and theories — were hardly of help in promoting the boldness and purity of the new works.

"No one dared simply to say that justification is to be found in the new European view, in a new ideology, and that we are already in the midst of a new conception which, sooner or later, will renew our art." In contrast to Kandinsky, for a long time Marc could not renounce the subject of his painting because the Creation was almost sacred to him. The animals, even more than man, personified for him the "universal oneness of the world." He found in them the "pure creature." This is why Marc so often chose animals as the subjects of his paintings. But he idealized them. What he depicts is the pure, the good, the untouched that they radiate. When he turned to abstract painting in 1913, Marc, although in agreement with Kandinsky's intellectual concept, reveals often enough in his crystalline planes, intermingling, vibrating forms, and fine color contrasts, a poetic transposition of his pantheistic enthusiasm.

August Macke, who was a most active collaborator in the formulation of the *Blue Riders Alamanac,* had received guidance and stimulation from the exhibitions of the New Artists Association, and especially from the paintings of Gabriele Münter and Alexej von Jawlensky. Macke shared this experience with Franz Marc, who was one of his close friends. Although his attitude toward art strongly differed from Kandinsky's and Marc's views — at least in the beginning — he later had much in common with the artists of the Blue Riders. "He was more naïve, but perhaps more talented too. Among all of us, it was he who gave color the brightest and purest tone, as clear and bright as his whole being," wrote Marc after the death of his friend. August Macke also strove to express reality directly, but he always felt the need for immediate visual experience. His meeting with Delaunay in 1912 influenced him decisively, and he found his own language and his shining, radiant color. Abstraction became for Macke a sort of pleasure to which he gave in now and then. His favored themes are strollers, girls under trees, slender women in front of fashion shop windows, harmonious couples, quiet lakes... He puts them into a kind of imaginary space of pure, glowing colors. Returning from a voyage to Tunis, which he had made in the company of Paul Klee in 1914 — a few months before the outbreak of the war — Macke brought back a number of aquarelles that were unique in their perfect grace and magnificence of colors.

For Paul Klee, who had joined the Blue Riders in 1912 but had always remained somewhat aloof, the journey to Africa was also of decisive importance. Prior to it, he had mostly done drawings; color had been almost meaningless to him. His scurrilous sketches, shown at the Tannhauser Gallery in Munich, had impressed Alfred Kubin, who in turn drew Kandinsky's attention to Klee. Both artists understood each other quickly. Kandinsky said later: "My neighbor in Schwabing was Paul Klee. At the time I met him, he was still very "small." But I can claim with justified pride that even then I sniffed in his little drawings (he did not paint yet) the big Klee of the future." The trip to Kairouan liberated Klee's poetic talent, freed his sparkling imagination from all shackles. "Color got me. I don't need to catch her. I know she has me forever. That is the meaning of the lucky hour: I and color are one. I am a painter," he wrote in his diary. The fact that color now became the ruling element of his work placed him right in the center of the artistic problems that concerned his friends in the Blue Riders. But the war brought soon an end to their joint efforts. Paul Klee, who was not drafted until 1916, let his work mature and made it bloom into unexpected beauty after the end of the war.

The only woman in the Blue Riders was Kandinsky's fourteen-year companion Gabriele Münter. Her painting suggests the influence of the Fauvists. Still lifes, flowers, and, most of all, landscapes are her themes. Gabriele Münter applied the contrast of pure colors as early as 1908, but never

with great vehemence. The importance of her artistic work lies in its expression. Armed with a naïve yet powerful certainty, she creates deep feelings out of brilliant simplicity.
Alexej von Jawlensky, who remained on friendly terms with the Blue Riders after they had left the New Artists Association, but who did not participate in their exhibitions, worked in a vein similar to that of Gabriele Münter. Jawlensky's painting is free and refreshing, his colors reveal a strong bond with the soil — a legacy of his native Russia. His themes are landscapes and particularly heads, which he painted with monumental simplicity. During World War I, Jawlensky's art grew more and more cerebral, and the human face became his only important subject.
The art of Lyonel Feininger, on the other hand, is totally different and his form of expression comes nearest to Klee. Feininger's special way of seeing made him also an excellent photographer. The Blue Riders, who had noted his singular talent, invited him to exhibit with them at the First German Autumn Salon in Berlin. The friendship of Kandinsky, Klee, Jawlensky, and Feininger survived World War I, and the artists later formed the Blue Four group.
Alfred Kubin who, together with Kandinsky, Marc, and Gabriele Münter, had been one of the original founders of the Blue Riders, worked exclusively as a pen-and-ink artist. His masterful drawings often show a demoniacal, spooky tendency. He illustrated numerous books.
The youngest member of the Blue Riders was the painter and graphic artist Heinrich Campendonck. His painting was influenced by Marc. He was especially esteemed because of his powerful and significant woodcuts.

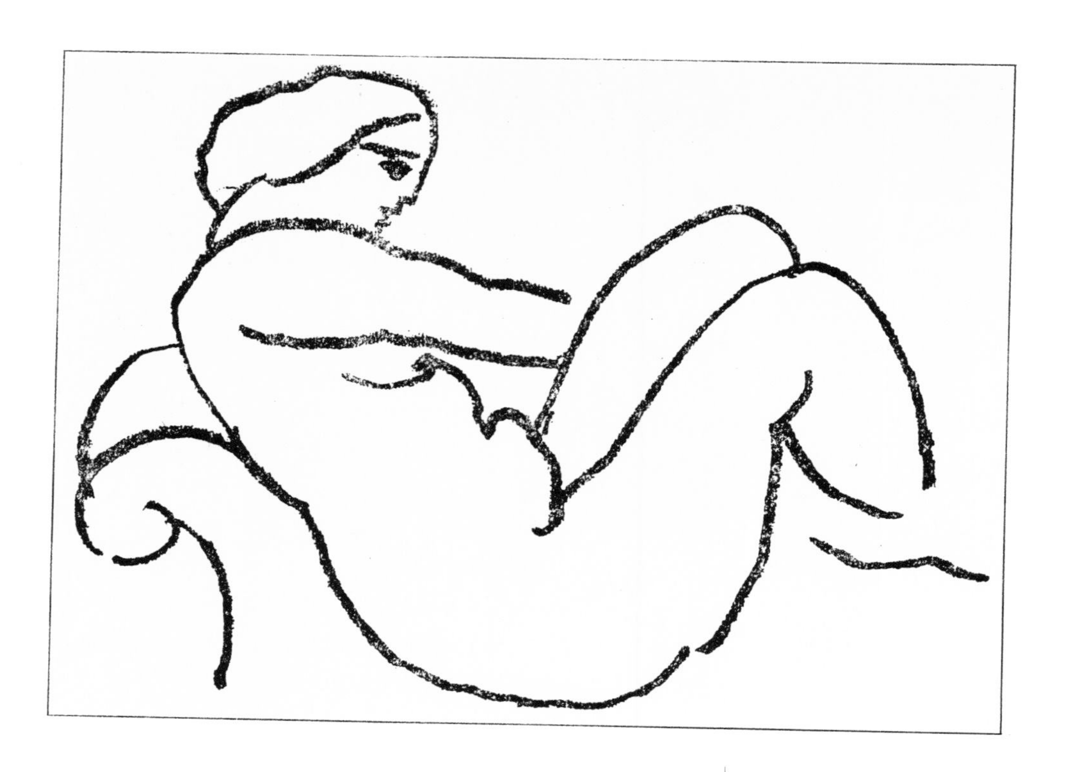

I

Alexej von Jawlensky

RED SHAWL

1909. Oil 20½ × 19 in. Modern Gallery Otto Stangl, Munich

Next to the landscape, the human face was the most interesting theme for Jawlensky. At the time the " Red Shawl " was painted, around 1909, Jawlensky was still tied to Russian folk art and its primitive power of expression. His glowing colors are applied with rich and deeply felt intensity. Even the woman's harshly introspective features, which suggest her Slavic origin, show the artist's earthiness. Between 1911 and 1914, Jawlensky concentrated his entire artistic work on the painting of heads, to which he gave more and more simplified and monumental forms. During the war his art developed a cerebral quality that endowed his models with almost mystic traits. In 1918 he turned to abstract painting.

Alfred Kubin, drawing.

II

Gabriele Münter

KANDINSKY AT THE TEA TABLE

1910 - 1911. Oil 27×19 in. Property of the artist

We see here Wassily Kandinsky, the intellectual leader of the Blue Riders through the eyes of his life's companion Gabriele Münter. With slightly inclined head, his eyes looking inward, he sits at the tea table. The black of his hair and beard continues along the strong contour line with which the artist separates the dark blue background against the shining blue of Kandinsky's jacket. As in many of her paintings since 1908, Gabriele Münter works here, too, with contrasting colors. Boldly she pits the green pot holder, with its rooster head and red comb, against the blue colors of the jacket and the background. Orange-colored fruit in a violet bowl rest on the dark green table, which is bounded to the right by the yellow wallpaper with its light-green and rose-colored patterns. In spite of their apparent contrasts, the colors of the painting blend into a single great melody.

III

Lyonel Feininger

BICYCLE RIDERS

1912. Oil 2 ft. 7 in. × 3 ft. 3 in. Ferdinand Möller Gallery, Cologne

In the work of Lyonel Feininger the essential is sharply observed; the observed, however, is subjected to a strict principle of order and built into the organic structure of the painting as so-to-speak "dematerialized reality." A finely balanced framework of lines, which reminds one of Klee, passes through the picture. Sometimes Feininger's paintings give the effect of irrational reflections. This is why it takes a second look to notice the five bicycle riders within the cubistic elements that characterize the structural form of the picture. The artist painted this work in 1912 after he had made the acquaintance of Delaunay. But one recognizes in the work, especially in the motif of motion, not only the Frenchman's influence; it also shows that he had been impressed by Futurism. The "Bicycle Riders" reveals the starting point of Feininger's own artistic language. The composition is a clear example of his modern form principles.

IV

Alexej von Jawlensky

MOUNTAINS (LANDSCAPE NEAR MURNAU)

1912. Oil 21×19 in. Collection Hanna Bekker vom Rath, Hofheim

The Russian painters who came to Munich around 1869 fell under the spell of Western painting and its influences. Jawlensky was deeply impressed by Cézanne and van Gogh, who showed him the way to simpler but also more expressive forms. In Murnau, where he and Marianne von Werefkin had settled at the same time as Kandinsky and Gabriele Münter, Jawlensky lost everything he had intended or learned at the sight of the powerful, towering mountains. Early impressions of Russian folk art and past dreams of color returned again. And so he executed his landscapes with great verve and in large patches of pure, brilliant colors that show the influence of Henri Matisse. All his landscapes, including the painting here, are of shining freshness and overwhelming vigor because of their simplicity.

V

Franz Marc

GAZELLE

1913. Tempera 15 × 17 in. Rhode Island Art School, Providence

Franz Marc strove to express in his paintings the closeness of the being with its essence and with the harmony of nature and the universe. He therefore preferred the animal to man, because it still remains — unlike man — in its original state. The external appearance of the represented animal does not matter. What counts is to bring out its inner being and its link with cosmic union. To accomplish this, Marc raises the animal above its natural existence and transfers it into an almost legendary sphere. The gazelle rests on a hill of triangles. A bundle of light rays seems to surround the animal like a halo. The tender, harmoniously balanced forms and the solemn and muted colors create a uniquely lyrical mood.

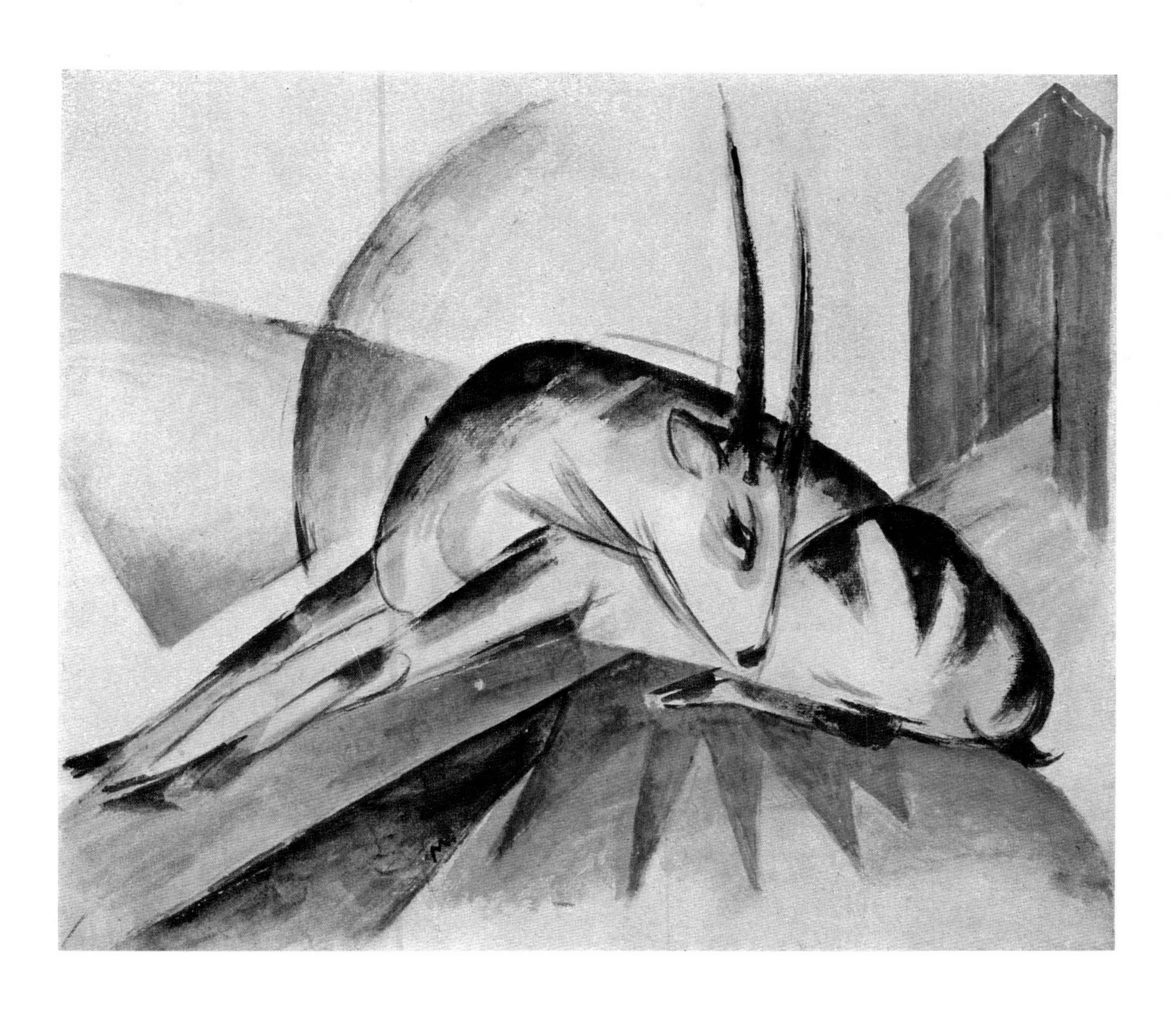

VI

August Macke

WALK ON THE BRIDGE

1913. Oil 20 × 22 in. Bernhard Köhler Collection, Berlin

In contrast to Kandinsky and Marc, August Macke did not look for abstraction. His principal theme was the human being, which he learned to represent with poetic power and perfect grace. His meeting with Delaunay, around 1912, greatly helped in his search of his own style and his gaining of "freedom over color." In the painting that we see here, the influence of Cubism on Macke is indicated in the already slightly simplified forms, while the brilliant colors with which he captures contemporary life show that he is also indebted to Futurism. His figures are beings of light and color. They affect us neither as inscrutable nor as demoniacal or erotic, but simply as human beings living their lives.

VII

Franz Marc

BATTLING FORMS

1914. Oil 3 ft. 2 in. × 4 ft. 3 in. Collections of Bavarian State Gallery, Munich

" I was encircled by strange forms and I drew what I saw: hard, soulless forms — black, steel-blue, and green ones — that blustered against each other." This is one of Franz Marc's aphorisms. It was perhaps the same vision that gave the artist the idea to his series of " gay," " playing," " battling," and " broken " forms that he created in 1914. The paintings of this group are completely abstract. The picture " Battling Forms " is based entirely on the color contrast between red and blue. The whirling " color monsters " seem to clash with thundering noise. Along the peripheral areas the two adversaries touch each other in twisting lines. Yellow tones, on the left side of the painting, illuminate the tumult of colors like flashing knife blades.

Klee
1914.57.

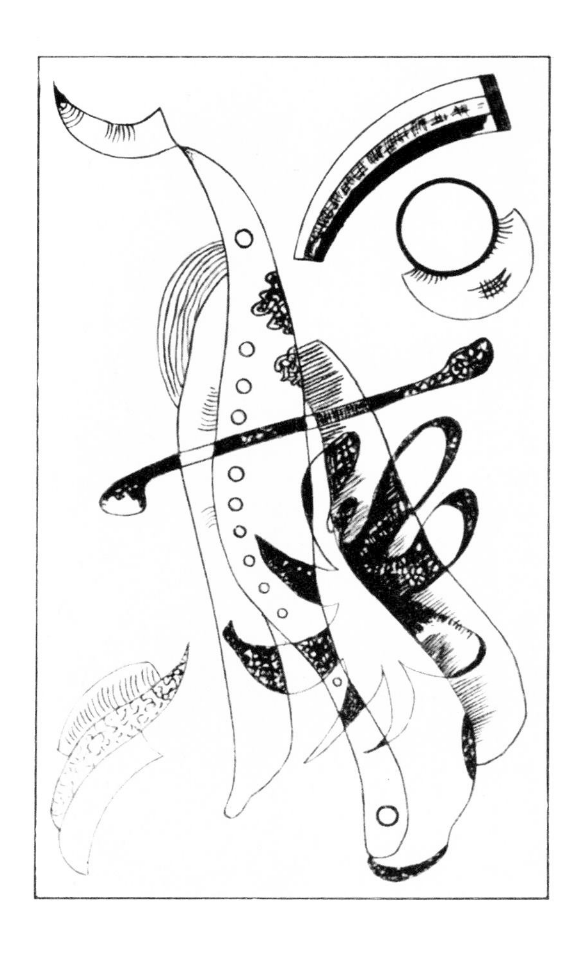

IX

Wassily Kandinsky

COMPOSITION

1914. Oil 3 ft. 3 in. × 2 ft. 6 in. The Solomon R. Guggenheim Museum, New York

Goethe's color doctrine states that colors have their own power of expression and can induce certain emotional reactions in human beings. Kandinsky had closely studied Goethe's work but it is claimed that he turned to abstractionism when he observed the strange harmony between a colorful dress and one of his paintings. Kandinsky created his first abstract painting in 1910 — the first abstract work that ever existed. The father of abstractionism called his non-objective sketches "improvisations," and the finally executed paintings "compositions." We see here a composition, conceived in 1914; its greatness lies in its lyrical coloration. Kandinsky manages by free association of non-objective, invented forms with colors that are liberated from all fetters to express a feeling or a state of mind.

X

Paul Klee

MASK

1940. Pastel and tempera 10½ x 13 in. Klee Foundation, Bern

The depth and breadth of Paul Klee's work is enormous. On the one hand, the artist gives rein to his imagination, which brings about daring and almost absurd forms; on the other, his creations are born of deep meditations over undreamed-of worlds, and change toward the end of his life into dark utterances. Frau Carola Giedion-Welcker, who visited Klee shortly before his death, wrote about his late work — to which the "Mask" belongs — that "the monumental paintings, gleaming like exotic runes, showed a heavy, black, and beamlike lineation on a covered color background which now had lost its transparency." She calls the last works of the artist "perhaps the greatest and most original contribution that Klee made to European art of the twentieth century."

BIOGRAPHIES

FEININGER Lyonel pp. 12, 13

Born in New York in 1871 of German parents, both practicing musicians, the artist was expected to follow in their footsteps, and was sent to Germany to further his musical education. But from 1887 to 1891 Feininger went instead to the Hamburg School of Applied Arts and the Berlin Academy of Painting. From 1891 to 1893 he finished his studies at the Colarossi Academy in Paris. In 1908 he moved to Berlin. After the war, Feininger was one of the most loyal supporters of the Bauhaus. Appointed in 1919 by Gropius to teach there, he remained until 1926, but maintained his relationship with the institute as a free-lance artist, after its move to Dessau and up to its closing in 1933. In 1937 Lyonel Feininger returned to America. He died in New York in 1956.

JAWLENSKY Alexej von 8, 9, 14, 15

Jawlensky was born in Souslowa, near Twer, in 1864. He began his studies in 1891 at the Moscow Academy and was also a pupil of the painter Repin. In 1896 he went to the painting school of Anton Azbe in Munich, where he met Kandinsky, and began to paint on his own in 1902. In 1909 he founded, together with Kandinsky and his friends, the New Artists Association. Jawlensky was in close contact with the Blue Riders, but did not take part in the group's exhibitions. In 1924, he founded, with Kandinsky, Klee, and Feininger, The Blue Four, who participated in several exhibitions in Germany and the United States. Alexej von Jawlensky died in Wiesbaden in 1941.

KANDINSKY Wassily 24, 25

Born in Moscow in 1866, Kandinsky was actually a jurist and economist, and decided only after he had reached his thirtieth year to become a painter. He went to Munich and studied at Azbe's painting school and with Franz Stuck at the Academy. Around 1900 he began to paint on his own. In 1902 he opened his own painting school and became president of an artists organization called Phalanx. He was a member of the German Artists Alliance, of the Berlin Secession, and of the Paris Autumn Salon. From 1903 to 1907 he visited Tunisia, Holland, Italy, and France. In 1909 he founded with like-minded painters the New Artists Association in Munich. In 1911 he and his friends resigned from this organization and formed the Blue Riders under his leadership. The two exhibitions of the group were held in 1911 and 1912. In the same year, Kandinsky's first collective exhibition took place at the "The Storm" Gallery in Berlin. In 1913 the publishing firm of the same name came out with a *Kandinsky Album* and the publisher Piper issued Kandinsky's *Sounds*. After the outbreak of the war, the artist went to Switzerland, moved in 1915 to Stockholm, and finally returned to Russia in the spring of 1916. In the wake of the Russian Revolution he held several important positions and taught at the Academy of Art and at the University. In 1921 he went back to Germany and the following year became professor at the Bauhaus in Weimar. There he formed, with Klee, Jawlensky, and Feininger, the Blue Four. In 1925 the Bauhaus moved to Dessau; in 1933 it was closed by the National Socialists. Kandinsky's paintings were confiscated and thrown away as "degenerate art." The painter went to Paris and participated there in the exhibitions of the *"Abstraction — Création Group."* In 1939 Kandinsky acquired French citizenship. He died in Neuilly-sur-Seine in 1944.

KLEE Paul 22, 23, 26, 27

Paul Klee, the first German painter since Dürer to attain worldwide importance, was born in Münchenbuchsee, near Bern, the son of a German musician. He studied in Munich from 1898 to 1901. Among his teachers was Stuck. In 1901, he journeyed to Italy. After marrying a pianist, he settled in Munich in 1906. In 1912, he joined the Blue Riders and in the same year met Picasso and Delaunay in Paris. From 1916 to 1918 Klee served as a soldier behind the front lines. In 1920, the Goltz Gallery in Munich arranged a big collective show of his works. In 1924, the artist became a member of the Blue Four. From 1921 to 1931 Paul Klee taught at the Bauhaus in Weimar and Dessau. In 1931, he was appointed professor at the Düsseldorf Academy where he remained until he was discharged in 1933. At the end of 1933 the artist returned to Switzerland and made his home in Bern. In 1937, 102 of his works were confiscated by the German government as "degenerate art" Paul Klee died in Muralto, a suburb of Locarno, in 1940.

KUBIN Alfred 10

Kubin was born in Leitmeritz, Bohemia, in 1877. In 1905 the artist traveled to Paris and visited Italy. In 1906 he acquired Zwickledt, an estate at the Inn River in Upper Austria, where he lived a secluded life until his death in 1959.

MACKE August 18, 19

The artist was born in Meschede on the Ruhr in 1887. From 1904 to 1906 he studied at the Düsseldorf Academy, and with Corinth in Berlin in 1907. After his marriage in 1909, Macke made his home in Bonn, but moved in the fall of 1910 to Tegernsee. There he became acquainted with Franz Marc, who brought him into the New Artists Association and introduced him to Kandinsky and his friends. In 1911 Macke stayed with Marc in Sindelsdorf and with Kandinsky in Murnau, and helped both friends in the preparation of the Blue Riders' *Almanac*. In 1912, he went with Marc to Paris where he met Delaunay, whose work made a deep impression on him. Macke was one of the organizers of the famous Special Alliance Exhibition, which was held in Cologne in 1912. In 1914 he traveled with Paul Klee and a Swiss painter to Tunisia From there he returned with aquarelles that are considered milestones of contemporary German art. August Macke enlisted in 1914 and was killed near Perthes, in the Champagne, in the second month of the war.

MARC Franz 16, 17, 20, 21

Franz Marc, who descended from a Munich artist family, was born in the Bavarian metropolis in 1880. He began his art studies in 1909 at the Munich Academy and studied at the same time with Hackl and Dietz. In the following years Marc traveled extensively. He went to Italy in 1903, to France in 1903, to Greece in 1906, and again to Paris in 1907, where he was greatly impressed by van Gogh's work. Until 1909 Franz Marc was still searching; only then did he find his own language and discovered, thanks to Macke, the form-giving laws of pure color. In 1910, the Brakl Gallery arranged his first one-man show. Shortly thereafter Marc met Kandinsky, with whom he founded the Blue Riders whose true exponent he became. His style had finally materialized and made him the best known and most popular modern German painter. Between 1911 and 1914 he created his best works, among them "Tower of the Blue Horses," "The Red Horses," and "Animal Destinies." The logical development of his art led Franz Marc in the end to abstract painting. At the outbreak of the war, he enlisted immediately. He was killed before Verdun in 1916.

MÜNTER Gabriele 11

Gabriele Münter was born in Berlin in 1877. From 1901 to 1902 she studied at the School of the Women Artists Society in Munich. In 1902 she became Kandinsky's pupil and remained his companion for many years. In 1908 the two artists acquired a house in Murnau. Gabriele Münter was a co-founder of the New Artists Association (1909) and of the Blue Riders in 1911, and participated in the First German Autumn Salon in 1913. In 1914 she accompanied Kandinsky to Switzerland, and in the following year they liquidated their household in Munich and moved to Stockholm. Kandinsky's return to Russia in 1916 ended their companionship. From 1918 to 1928 Gabriele Münter lived in Copenhagen, but often traveled to Munich, Murnau, Cologne, Berlin, and to the Italian and Swiss Alps. From 1929 to 1930 she lived in France and finally settled in Murnau in 1931. She still lives in the house that she had shared with Kandinsky. Lately the artist, who had fallen into oblivion for a long time, regained her deserved recognition.